FLASH POEMS

FLASH POEMS

POETRY AND PROMPTS

Second Sunday Goes Fourth
Writing Group
Lawrence, Kansas

Published in 2018 by Anamcara Press LLC
Contributors: © 2018 by Deborah Altus, Micki Carroll, Iris Craver, Kimberli Eddins, Louie Galloway, Katherine Greene, Sandy Hazlett, Joanne C. Hickey, Nancy Hubble, Dixie Lubin, Ronda Miller, Amy Nixon, Gail Curtis Sloan, Libeth Tempero.

Cover Photograph © 2018 by Tim Passmore, Lightning strike in Republic County, Kansas 2016

Book design by Maureen Carroll
Palatino Linotype, Ostrich Sans Rounded, Tsisquilisda, We are Depraved
Printed in the United States of America.

Book Description: *Flash Poems* offers an anthology of poems and the prompts that inspired them. These 100-plus thought-provoking prompts will help you manage writer's block and have fun in creative exploration.

All rights reserved. No part of this publication may be reproduced, distributed, or transmitted in any form or by any means, including photocopying, recording, or other electronic or mechanical methods, without the prior written permission of the publisher, except in the case of brief quotations embodied in critical reviews and certain other noncommercial uses permitted by copyright law. For permission requests, write to the publisher, addressed "Attention: Permissions Coordinator," at the address below.

ANAMCARA PRESS LLC
P.O. Box 442072, Lawrence, KS 66044
https://anamcara-press.com

Ordering Information:
Quantity sales. Special discounts are available on quantity purchases by corporations, associations, and others. For details, contact the publisher at the address above.
Orders by U.S. trade bookstores and wholesalers. Please contact Ingram Distribution.

Publisher's Cataloging-in-Publication data
Carroll, M, Editor
Flash Poems/ M Carroll

ISBN-10: Flash Poems 1-941237-17-7

ISBN-13: Flash Poems 978-1-941237-17-5

[1. POE000000 POETRY / General. 2. REF020000 REFERENCE / Research. 3. POE024000 POETRY / Women Authors.]

DEDICATION

We dedicate this book to Iris Craver for her courage and resourcefulness, for never giving up; to Caryn Miriam Goldberg, Kelley Hunt, and the Brave Voice participants for their continued encouragement; and to Katherine Greene and Dan Bentley who have provided us with amazing energy and unfailing support in the form of a warm, comfortable place to write!

CONTENTS

FOREWORD xi
PROMPTS 1
POEMS 5
Deborah Altus 6
Micki Carroll.................................... 17
Iris Craver 29
Kimberli Eddins 38
Louie Galloway 41
Katherine Greene 48
Sandy Hazlett 56
Joanne C. Hickey............................. 64
Nancy Hubble 72
Dixie Lubin 83
Ronda Miller................................... 95
Amy Nixon.................................... 102
Gail Curtis Sloan 104
Libeth Tempero 106
CONTRIBUTORS 111

FOREWORD

This collection of unedited poems inspired by prompts and written in ten to fifteen minutes represents many pleasant Sunday afternoons at the Second Sunday Goes Fourth writing group. Iris Craver, the founder of the group, was leading a poetry writing group for inmates at the Douglas County Jail, and she thought it would be fun to also have a community writing group. We meet on the second and fourth Sundays from 2 to 4 p.m., thus the name Second Sunday Goes Fourth. There are usually 6 to 10 writers around the table.

Our rules are simple. No self-deprecation is allowed. We don't critique others' writings. Appreciation and enthusiasm are encouraged. We keep a bowl full of writing prompts to which we all contribute. When the pens are laid down we read around the table. Reading is always optional. One of our great pleasures is listening to what each of us has written and to see how our approaches are similar or different. There are always poems that are breathtaking in each round.

We hope you enjoy these poems and try your hand at writing from the prompts. You can use the prompts provided, or even pull a line from any of the poems to get you started in a flash! If any reader is interested in starting a community writing group, let us know by contacting the publisher. Have fun!

Second Sunday Goes Fourth

PROMPTS

1. A Lullaby
2. A Memory Still Charded With Threat
3. All At Once
4. A Moth In The Salt
5. Appalachian Woman
6. Apples
7. As I Turned The Corner, I Saw The Car
8. A Snowy Evening
9. Asparagusto
10. Bedtime Story
11. Beautiful Women
12. Beside The River Of Dance, The Trees Seek
13. Between Seasons
14. Blank Prompt
15. Burn It Up
16. Celebrate Celibacy
17. Change Will Come
18. Children Grow Up, Leave
19. Coils And Curls
20. Colossus
21. Confession
22. Cornered Erosion
23. Crackerjack Sweetheart
24. Dad
25. Drenched To The Bone
26. Earth And Sky
27. Eliminate
28. Ferment
29. Finding Joy In Hard Times
30. Flying In Dreams
31. Food Haiku
32. Free Writing Ignoring The Prompt
33. Geese

34. Genius Is 99% Perspiration
35. Glued Together
36. Hand Me Downs
37. Her His Presence
38. Honey
39. Hospice
40. How Language Shapes Our Thinking
41. I Forgot When
42. I Have Fattened Into My Mother's Age
43. I Held The Clay
44. I Lie Sleepless
45. I Made A Decision
46. Immortality
47. In The Dark
48. I Stand
49. It's Simple
50. It Was A Holy Moment, An Unexpected Moment
51. Killing Time
52. Lady Holds The Bird
53. Landscape Of My Heart
54. Let Us Have A Moment Of Silence
55. Lifesaver
56. Listening Deep
57. Look!
58. Lost And Found
59. Men At 50
60. Misty Car Window
61. Motherhood
62. Mother Needs You
63. My Chosen Landscape
64. Now And Then
65. Now The Earth With Many Flowers Puts On Her Spring Embroidery - Sappho
66. Oh That Sweet, Sweet Ass
67. Our Animal Has Never Bitten Anyone Before
68. Out Of Balance
69. Perhaps Your Wolf Has Done All She Can For You & Has Moved On

70. Picture Of A Woodcarving With The Caption, "Man At Podium"
71. Please. More Squeeze
72. Pop Explosion
73. Red. Dirt. Alley
74. Ripe Fruit
75. Root Veggies
76. Salt & Pepper
77. Scraps Of Your Life
78. Seven of Pentacles
79. She Says
80. Shudda, Cudda, Wudda
81. Sitting In A Dark House Of Pain
82. Sky And Air, Earth And Water
83. Sleep Walking
84. Sonnet, Iambic Pentameter, 14 lines
85. Snake
86. Spirals
87. Spring Fever
88. Standing Above Them
89. Strength Of Night
90. Tabs
91. Teakettle
92. Terminal Nostalgia
93. Thaw
94. The Best Chocolate Cake
95. The Danger Of Dictionaries
96. The One That Got Away
97. The Landscape Of Time
98. The Last Time I Danced
99. The Process Of Extinction
100. The Young
101. This Might Be True... Or Not
102. Turning Point
103. Umbilical Cord
104. Vision
105. Waiting For A Change
106. Waking Up

107. Welcome To The House Of…
108. What I Hear In Silence
109. What The Magpie Saw
110. What Song Is Stuck In Your Head
111. What The River Told Me
112. When Dragons Fly
113. When I Saw You In The…
114. Whispered Into My Ear
115. Whose Garlic
116. Wide Open
117. Wild Sunflower
118. Winter Mice
119. Wreckage
120. Write A Poem About A Specific Tree
121. Write A Poem With As Few Adjectives As Possible
122. Women At The Well Or Quenching Our Thirst
123. Word Salad
124. Write A Short Poem About A Vegetable Or Fruit
125. You Can't Go Back
126. You Do Not Have To Be What You Are Not

POEMS

PROMPT: MOTHERHOOD

The mothers of my childhood
wore gold lamé sandals
with fuchsia-colored nails
and tight perms finished
with Clairol rinses to hide the gray;
wore culottes in wash-n-wear fabric
and sensible lightly padded bras
that clasped in the back.

The mothers of my childhood
drove massive wood-paneled station wagons
with three rows of bench seats and
an extra pop-up seat in the back
for the oops child – the one left behind at
filling stations that gave green stamps—
stamps that the mothers of my childhood
carefully pasted into books and traded for
toasters or whisks or other gadgets
to whip powdered potatoes into
fluffy peaks or turn Rice-a-Roni
into a San Francisco Treat.

The mothers of my childhood
had tiny waists, big hair, and
voluminous purses filled with everything
they'd need to win on Let's Make a Deal
or to fix a bloody knee.

The mothers of my childhood
went to every PTA meeting,
baked casseroles for new neighbors
and elderly shut-ins,
made covered dishes for church suppers and
sat through every concert, play, ballet
and sing-along the school could invent.

The mothers of my childhood
ironed, mopped, swept and dusted
but never worked and didn't sweat.
They blended with the wallpaper
except when mocked by a cocky adolescent
or yelled at by an angry husband.

The mothers of my childhood
are mostly gone now,
the remaining few accessorized by
walkers, canes, wheelchairs and catheters.
They are slipping away as
quietly as they lived,
decomposing under the very ground
they once tended.

The mothers of my childhood.

~ Deborah Altus

PROMPT: PICTURE OF A WOODCARVING WITH THE CAPTION "MAN AT PODIUM"

Man at podium
speaks ad nauseum
drones ad infinitum
but I am done.
Done with podiums
and men who rise to them.
Take your odium
and be gone.

~ Deborah Altus

PROMPT: TURNING POINT

She looked so small
and sweet
and innocent
sitting there in her orange jumpsuit
that I wanted to hug her,
take her home,
feed her comfort foods,
tuck her in and sing her
a lullaby.
What was her turning point?
She told the police
she just wanted to see
what it was like to kill
someone
and she did just that.
Slit his throat and
left a message in
his blood
on the wall.
Was she psychotic?
A victim of abuse?
The victim of a society gone wrong?
Something else entirely?
The news was full
of conjecture.
What was her turning point?
She passed me a note,
thanking me for
welcoming her into
the jail writing class,
for being warm, friendly,
and smart (her words).

She looked so small
and sweet
and innocent
sitting there in her orange jumpsuit.
What was her turning point?

~ Deborah Altus

PROMPT: ROOT VEGGIES

Turnips
parsnips
potatoes
and peas
throw me a knife
a skillet
some cheese
a pinch of dill
a handful of parsley
a dash of salt
toss it all nicely

Mince some garlic
caramelize onions
add the rutabaga
almost done, then
gather the family
the forks
and the plates
eat it while hot
don't be late!

~ Deborah Altus

PROMPT: WRITE A POEM WITH AS FEW ADJECTIVES AS POSSIBLE

I like to walk
with my dog
on the levee
in the morning
when the sun is
rising over the river and
skip when no one is looking,
toss a stick for the dog or
throw rocks in
the river so I can
hear them plop
and watch the rings
form and disappear,
form and disappear
in the water
in the morning
when the sun is
rising over the river.

I like to sit
with my dog
on the levee
in the morning
when the sun is
rising over the river
and watch the boats
filled with women
glide past as the man
in the back yells
"stroke, stroke, stroke"
and their arms move
back and forth,

back and forth
in the water
in the morning
when the sun is
rising over the river.

~ Deborah Altus

PROMPT: COILS AND CURLS

Ribbons on presents
little girls' hair
daffodil petals
smoke in the air

Tails on piglets
snakes in the grass
thinly sliced ginger
roads near a pass

Springs on a door
pasta on plates
ringlets on toddlers
cats on a grate

Curls and coils
and circumnavigation
around and around
in wild rotation

Beautiful curves
marvelous twists
why do it straight?
come on – take a risk!

~ Deborah Altus

PROMPT: THE BEST CHOCOLATE CAKE

Some cakes are made
in sheet pans
bundt pans
or spring-form pans
but the best chocolate cake
is made in 9-inch rounds –
three to be exact –
to allow enough frosting
in each bite.

Some cakes are frosted
in lemon
vanilla
or cream cheese
but the best chocolate cake
is frosted in
deep rich chocolate
thickly spread between
each layer and
over the top and sides.

Some cakes are good
when they are
doughy
flakey
or crumb-like
but the best chocolate cake
is moist –
moist enough to
dissolve in your mouth
with only the swirl of
your tongue.

Some cakes are made
from recipes in
magazines
cookbooks
or the Internet
but the best chocolate cake
is made from a
chocolate-stained recipe card
written in the hand of your
mother
grandmother
or aunt.

Some cakes are made
in bakeries
or restaurants
or cafeterias
but the best chocolate cake
is made at home
where children clamor
to lick the beaters
and the bowls.

The best chocolate cake
is so much more than cake.
The best chocolate cake
is made from
legacy
memory
and love.

~ Deborah Altus

PROMPT: MOTHER'S ADVICE

Mother's Advice: A to Z
Always
be
captivating.
Don't
eat
fingernails.
Iron
jerseys,
keeping
low
moisture.
Never
ogle
publicly.
Quickly
repent
sins.
Type
unerringly.
Value
wisdom.
eXcite
your
Zeus!

~ Deborah Altus

PROMPT: WORD SALAD

Some words are so beautiful
I'd like to scoop them
off the page and
feast on their loveliness:
Cerulean
Parmigiana
Serengeti.
Or better yet, toss
them into a salad with
a fine olive oil and
aged balsamic vinegar with
a twist of black pepper and
a light grating of aged cheese
for brunch alone on
a screened-in porch with
a dog at my feet and
sunlight on my shoulders.
If words only had calories, I'd
choose them for dinner
every time.

~ Deborah Altus

PROMPT: LADY HOLDS THE BIRD

She sits at her perch
on the sunroom sofa
watching the birds
dance back and forth from
feeder to bird bath,
only seconds at each place.
They tease her with
the lift of a wing,
a bit of leg,
a show of breast,
and then they're off,
moving like she used to
when she chopped onions
or ran after toddlers.
She envies their speed;
They, her repose.

~ Deborah Altus

PROMPT: APPALACHIAN WOMAN
Sparrow Song Girl

Appalachian woman
Singing clear as sparrow's song
Plaintive
I, seeking cure, a spur
A conjure
Or conjurer
Just a bit o' power
Over circumstance
Life waving in the wind
Like the flag-of-chance
Turn-of-wheel
Fortune-spill.

Appalachian woman
Held out her hand
Took a stand
How could i not reach for
The life line
An omen, a sign
Double-life woman
Sparrow song girl
Woman with cure
Who knows how to soar
Collects a wisp of hair, a drop of blood
A conjurer.

Never young at 17
Elemental search
For me
Wanting just to be free
She a simple woman
Strong

Smoked a bong
One hit, or two
Don't be greedy
Hold your own, don't be needy
Few knew her double-life
One seemingly of strife
Or just a joyful release
From bull-shit-ery
She invited me
A caldron of ideas bore scrutiny.

She took me to her secret cove
A book filled nook
An easy-breezy special space
A place of one who lived in grace
The cat upon the windowsill
Nudged my hand
As she read a spell
From some old volume and showed me more
Intellectual witch who knows the score
She thanked her grandma and her ma
Then took me back through generations in time
To an Appalachian state of mind.

Old recipes handed down
Tried and true
Silent and full of sound
A bit of practical
Magical dust to tie together
To add some trust
A wisp of hair, a drop of blood
To keep us well, to stop the flood
A bone, a feather, a scrap of cloth
Perhaps the wing of a night-hawk moth
Tied together with care and string
Can bring about most anything.

Appalachian woman
Double-life woman
Real as Sparrow's song
Woman with cure
Conjurer
Who knows how to right a wrong
Taught me to soar
To roar
To combine
A bone, a feather, a scrap of cloth
To pass along
Wisdom strong
And hold it dear
Like Sparrow's song.

~ Micki Carroll

PROMPT: SLEEPWALKING
Don Juan's Daughter

Sleepwalking through life
Through love
Eyes half shut and glazed
Wandering, drifting
Listless
Like a bee flitting, feelinglessly
Landing lightly
Avoiding exposure
Avoiding awakening
Slipping easily into the warmth of evening
A revealing silken dress
The rapture of unknowingness
Reaching out with lips and arms
Beyond the searing pain of
Right or wrong
Into the night.

~ Micki Carroll

PROMPT: LOST AND FOUND

I lost myself in academia
    Wrapped in others words
    Cloaked in awkward ideas
    & thoughts that never quite fit
When all was silent on the shore
I faced myself and found much more
And all the repetitious lines
Had formed deep grooves worn with time

I lost myself in compensated labor
    Working for the man
    Draped in others desires
    Lost inside their plan
When the labor was no more
I faced myself and found I'd scored
And all the mindless rules
Demeaningly unnecessary had become mine.

I lost myself in children's chatter
    Diapers on the floor
    A sesame street of flowing ideas
    Often nothing more
When goodbyes were said and done
I sat in silence and alone
And all the thoughts of anguished cries
And laughter filling up the skies
Became the fuel for future dreams.

~ Micki Carroll

PROMPT: BESIDE THE RIVER OF THE DANCE THE TREES SEEK

Beside the River of the Dance the Trees seek
Rhythm
That pulsing rhythm rising rising from the pumping/sucking absorption
Deep from the earth
The spring of life flowing up from the roots
And the leaves sway in the breeze

Beside the River of Dance the Trees seek expression
That sometimes babbling bubbling exuberant expression
we humans take for granted – meaningless muttering – that
Trees propel magically, silently
Listen, you'll hear what they say

Beside the River of Dance the Trees seek Connection
That throbbing, pulsating electricity that jumps
From you to me
And also to the Tree
To the center of our community
Lo these many centuries
The tree of life that caries our dreams
As we sing together beside the River of Dance.

~ Micki Carroll

PROMPT: KILLING TIME
Temps Mort

I killed the time recklessly (viciously?)
Stabbing with my lethargy
Prodding with my apathy
Parrying left and right
Shoulds and oughts
Sending them flying like so many fleas
Like nags – those demands
I make of myself.

I killed the time with glee
Gloating over the demise of productivity
Wallowing in sticky-sweet lazy
Floating neither left nor right
Floating free
Sending thoughts like balloons in the air
Then popping each
Joyfully.

I killed the time rather than watch it fly
I mortify
Embalming words in stones of imperfection
Freezing thought in midair
Then watching the letters drop and break like silent glass
Shards flying, stabbing
Embedding my consciousness
Creating kaleidoscope

Starting the process anew
Damn, where's a pen, my camera, a drum?
Inspiration!
Such joy in creation.
Not lost
Not undone.

~ Micki Carroll

PROMPT: LIFESAVER

A river snakes across the valley floor
Weaving pools and marshes
Leaving traces for tadpoles to hatch and
Birds for prey to hunt

It meanders in a general direction
Never alone but always in connection
Never the same but always changing
Creating patterns
Creating life
Winding this way and that as
The land shifts, as the
Weather changes.

It has been a lifesaver
This river of nuance
Of chance
It defines the character of the people
As much as it defines the character of the land
Leaving permanent marks
Scaring the earth
As it scarred my arms when I tangled with the rocks it carries
Etching an imprint of distinction
Molding fine mountains
And my life.

~ Micki Carroll

PROMPT: POP EXPLOSION

What is the direction of the grain
Of the wood of the spoon
Worn smooth by the grip of your hand as it
Mixes and blends sweet and sour
Light and dark
Making magic tastes
Miracle tarts

What is the direction of the clouds
In the sky
Billowing pillows piled high and
Crowded like popcorn overflowing
A bountiful blue bowl

What is the direction of the story you tell
In your melodious voice
Colorful strands that you
Weave so well in and out
Up and down
Carrying the listener all around

What is the direction of this planet we're on
Turning in circles
Following the sun
Where are the sign posts
That say when to run
Have we gone too far
Can our mistakes be undone?

~ Micki Carroll

PROMPT: THE PROCESS OF EXTINCTION
The Origin Of Birds

It happens
this process of extinction
that morphs into
transformation

the large femur bones
shrink to minisculty
carpals turn to claws
clavicles to wishbones
      desiring weightlessness
bones fuse to become beak
      face-fingers to feed the young

Theropod dinosaur, Tyrannosaurus rex
shrinks to fit the size of his tiny brain

Velvetine Velociraptor
Lunching on lizards in the Mesozoic era
grows wings
flies into a very different future

Hopeful monsters
some said
but now we understand
evolution didn't create birds
dinosaurs created a burst of evolution
bloomed feathers
and awkwardly stumbled
into free soaring flight.

~ Micki Carroll

PROMPT: SPIRALS

Spirals turning twisting
Up and down
Toward the center
Round and round

Spirals spinning energy
With intelligence
And collectively
Ever higher
Together bound

Spirals picking up the dust
Pulling into form
With momentum and
Synergistically

Spirals were first discovered
On grey stones deep underground
Fluorescently marking the way
For the intrepid
To follow

Be brave now
Crouch upon your belly
Keep your head low
Crawl like a snake
Yes. It is dark and tight and arduous
and steep and scary and triumphant
As you gain little by little a few feet
And then yards

This tunnel is long
But keep your beam on the spirals
Keep centered
Keep moving
Keep faith

Soon and suddenly
You'll break free into the wild open cave of Lascaux
And the jaguar will greet you and
You will be born into a new life

You will have spiraled to a new dimension
And at this new level
Your eyes will open wider
From here
You can look down the long trail
You have traversed

The trail that brought you to this
Place of power
See how it twists
Back upon itself spiraling
Down towards incomprehension
Here
Understanding
You acknowledge
The spiral of existence.

~ Micki Carroll

PROMPT: WHISPERED INTO MY EAR
The Voices of Stones

The voices of stones
Speak the language of the ages
Pellucid crystal
Mutable ruby
Combustible kimberlite
Quixotic quartz

The voices of stones
Are culled in the inner flame
Through rapid oxidation
Scintillating, sparkling
Growing at angles
Pullulating

The voices of stones
Are freed by their name
Bursting outward and finally identified
Breccia, Evaporite, Fanglomerate, Gneiss -
Lucent and transpicuous
Whispering stardust.

~ Micki Carroll

PROMPTS: MY CHOSEN LANDSCAPE/ BETWEEN SEASONS

There is no escape from this land where I live.
I checked the Canadian immigration website weeks ago
before it crashed
and I am eligible.
I'm one of the privileged few that if I chose to, I could flee
and then where would I be?
My family and friends left behind?
With stories about a grandmother in the autumn season of
life who ran away?
There is no escape from this life I chose,
extending myself widely and deeply like the heritage
tomatoes in my garden
creeping vines hiding babies under leaves so that next year,
next season,
new ones sprout from a single seed.
I choose to stay in this place and wear an apron as my shield
for the battle,
Pile up books to build a fortress,
And use my love as a weapon of mass instruction.

~ Iris Craver

PROMPT: MOTHER NEEDS YOU

Mother needs to bleed
Mother needs water to clean up messes and cook cabbage stew, too.
"Read the signs," Mother says, "take heed."
I've told you time and time again, "pay attention".
Is the wind rattling your windows and doors?
Does it sound like the trains hauling the remains pulled from my veins?
Mother feels such pain
Baby girl caught on fire, never the same
Mother smells like seed potatoes
She sees the petunia blossom in the brick patio crack
Mother carries the book of ages on her back
Mother laughs in my eyes

~ Iris Craver

PROMPTS: ALL AT ONCE/ MISTY CAR WINDOW

I was driving down the street, routine, and all at once,
this squirrel ran right out in front of my car.
I swerved, but felt the awful clunk.
I looked in the rear view mirror at its twitching body,
almost dead.
It was a clear day, no rain, no misty car windows.
A clear day and I killed a squirrel.
I killed a squirrel.
Last time, I killed a dog.
That was 40 years ago.
I was on my way to work at the psychiatric hospital.
I hit that dog with my car and flashes of that dead dog still
run through my mind
like the delusions of the psychotic patient I work with who
thought he was a chicken
or the other lady who kept pebbles in cupcake tins all
around her bed
and called them her babies.
I killed a dog.
My stomach hurts when I think about that dog
and that squirrel.
It must be fucking horrible to be a soldier.

~ Iris Craver

PROMPT: I FORGOT WHEN

She remembered what it was like to run down the sidewalk
not noticing the world flying by
and then stopping, just like that, to sit for an hour searching
for a 4-leaf clover.
Magical, it seemed magical to find that spot where luck grew
and she would gather these green gems
and press them carefully in a Nancy Drew book, "The Secret
of the Lost Lock".
She remembered what it was like to hide a coffee can
full of treasures
(a pen knife, matches, needle and thread, buttons, a candle
and a pack of Wrigley spearmint gum)
in the fork of the tree down along the railroad tracks
near the shack where the bums lived.
No one knew she spent time down there sitting 'round
the campfire in the late afternoon,
listening to the hobos sing and tell stories,
drinking Mad Dog 20 20 and smoking Camel cigarettes.
They were so kind to her and cautioned her
not to tell her mother
or she wouldn't be able to come around anymore.
So she kept this secret part of her life tucked away,
like a dream.
She remembered the park nearby where the fairies
made rings in the grass.
She knew about fairy rings 'cause her mama had told her.
Sometimes she figured that since mama knew about fairies
and lucky 4- leaf clovers,
she might be OK about the bum shack too,
but she loved the men down by the track too much to risk it.

She remembered when mama noticed something missing
from the house
(like the jar of safety pins that she'd taken to add
to the coffee can).
She'd tell mama, must be the little people who took it.
Mama would smile.
Of course, of course.
The little people.
The little people.

~ Iris Craver

PROMPT: FERMENT

The linoleum on the kitchen floor was worn down
on the path
where she paced,
day and night,
concocting elixirs and salves and fermented mulberry juice
for when the fevers sat in.
Her medicine cabinet was the breezeway where chamomile
and basil
and mullein hung in bunches to dry.
Down the rickety steps was her wooden chair where she'd
sit in the sun
grinding fennel seeds with a mortar and pestle to
add to the tea
brewing in the pot on the stove
for that time of the month when her visitor cramped her
doubled up
and she'd leave spots of blood on the threshold of the door
where she stood wringing her hands
hoping no one had seen her reading palms for that lady
down at the beauty salon.
She knowd what was beyond the veil.
She knowd it all her life.

~ Iris Craver

PROMPT: WIDE OPEN

Put the power here and open your heart, wide open
Connect to all that is and open your beingness, wide open
See beyond what seems to be and open your eyes,
wide open
Create what calls out to you and open your life, wide open
Open the doors, the windows, the cabinets, the books,
the drawers,
the jars, the thoughts, the toilet, the song, the box,
the paint can,
the photo album, the street, the water spigot, the laptop,
the vise, the email,
the map, the world , the universe, the galaxy, open,
open wide.

~ Iris Craver

PROMPT: SHUDDA, CUDDA, WUDDA

I shudda paid more heed to my mama, don't ya know
She kept all the herbs and how to make them grow
She was wise and oh, so ever sad
I gave her hell, such a nasty young girl, I was bad, really bad
I cudda spent more time helping her sow her seeds
She was kinda crippled and it was hard for her to see
Instead, I slammed the door hard as I took my leave
to go down the alley and smoke a little weed
I wudda liked a "do over", but she don't even visit me
in my dreams.
The best I can do now is take my grandbabies
down to the garden, it seems.

~ Iris Craver

PROMPT: NOW AND THEN

Now and then, time changes and there's no figuring how.
It happens unexpectedly.
Running late, I need to be somewhere across town
in 10 minutes
and yet I arrive 5 minutes early.
When I flew to New Zealand, I landed the day before I left
(or was it the other way around?).
I like deja vu when you get to do the same exact moment
over again.
Time changes and even the clocks don't know why.
Aboriginal people have no words for past or future,
even so, I've visited both places.
There was that time long ago
when I was thrown off a cliff by the villagers
for being a witch
And the other time long from now
when I am teaching the young ones how to put up tomatoes.
Now and then, time changes and yet the sun
comes up every day.
Once, I lost all track of time......I fell in love.
My daddy build a grandfather's clock.
I never could get it to work after he died.
Time had changed.
Every so often, time almost stands still
And then I blink and time changes
And I breathe and time changes
And my heart beats and time changes.

~ Iris Craver

PROMPT: A LULLABY

Let my tired old arms cradle you, dear
Let my tired old voice sing a song for you to hear
Let my tired old eyes close now as we gently rock
Let my tired old heart love you round and around the clock

Let me hold you to keep
Let me sing you a song
Let me rock your eyes to sleep
Let me love you all night long

Let my tired old knees jiggle you, my dear
Let my tired old ears hear your little tears
Let my tired old hand pat you in the breeze
Let my tired old angels smile on you, please

Let me keep you from the bumps
Let me hear you softly hum
Let me hold you through your life
Let me love you through the night

~ Iris Craver

PROMPT: DRENCHED TO THE BONE

She didn't have sense to come in out of the rain
She hardly used an umbrella,
though she carried one just the same
Drenched to the bone felt like coming home
Back in the womb
Jump in a lake, her favorite sort of date
Sit on the porch when it storms
Hail, yes!
Gales and buckets,
gutters and seams,
thunder and lightning,
dilated eyes in a dream
Drenched to the bone
Chilled cells gulping,
fingers wrinkled like prunes,
glorious nature,
throwing love from the moon
Pulling her heart tides
Calming her inside
Water wells, rainbows tell
Bones dancing in the rain
No need to explain

~ Iris Craver

PROMPT: UMBILICAL CORD
Throw Out the Life Line

Throw out the life line for the umbilical cord has been cut
A life time ago.
Throw out the life line because the telephone line is too thick
With party lines and too busy to reach 911.
Throw out the life line but first, press one for English,
2 for Spanish or zero for someone who might care.
Throw out the life line, she's up on the high wire
And forgot her tiny flowered umbrella.
Back and forth she sways. Steady. Stop.
She scoops herself up in a breath... foot slowly slides...
Forward step.. slow-w-w, step.. slow- w.
Throw OUT the life line she doesn't need it today.

~ Kimberli Eddins

PROMPT: WILD SUNFLOWERS

Summer recedes,
Cool wind gusts chasing fallen debris,
Sun tucked in cloud quilts covering and uncovering,
Peek-a-boo,
Wild sunflowers burn hot yellow.

~ Kimberli Eddins

PROMPT: LISTENING DEEP

Insomnia
Insomnia,
Brain strain,
Thought spot,
Replay same day,
Wired and wilted,
Heightened, frightened,
Sleep,
Good luck!

~ Kimberli Eddins

PROMPT: A SNOWY EVENING

Foot goes side to side.
Hand sweeps across the page to start a new line.
Fruit rests quietly in table, waiting.
Pens like soldiers, lined up on writing surface.
My other pair of glasses ready to give me different eyes
To see my words.

~ Kimberli Eddins

PROMPT: APPLES

Apples in a plastic bag,
Just don't seem right or natural,
Sweet fragrant prisoners.

~ Kimberli Eddins

PROMPT: LISTENING DEEP

Creative spirit in morning darkness,
Whispers guiding my hand,
Lines and curves speak themselves onto the canvas.
Awareness in freedom, I let go again and again,
Trusting.
I am awakening from once dulled slumber,
Now laughing in my sleep,
My eyes flutter to see.
I am
Full
Juicy
Ripe
Holy

~ Kimberli Eddins

PROMPT: FOOD HAIKU

I yam that I yam
Not broccoli. Not cabbage
I yam that I yam

~ Louie Galloway

PROMPT: WHAT THE RIVER TOLD ME

I have lots of brothers and sisters running around.
They try to keep orderly but sometimes they get too big for
their bridges- and that makes a mess.
I'm the biggest. I've been around the longest.

I remember when those steam boat captains pleaded with
me. "Take it easy. Go slow" Or sometimes "I'm late. Go
fast." But it's the little guys I have to watch out for.

Now you know my name: "Mighty Mississippi." Biggest guy
and gal (I'm both) around.
I take everything and I give back.
I'll feed you. You can count on me.

But you've got to stop feeding me those factory spill overs.
I talked to the EPA, but I hear
they're going out of business.

You people think you know it all
but you don't. I'll probably do better without you, though I
like your songs. They go with my gurgling.

~ Louie Galloway

PROMPT: FINDING JOY IN HARD TIMES

She lived up the hill from me, a clay dirt road
as most of our roads were in that small Southern town.
She was often not at home, or at least seemed so
as knocking doors produced much of nothing.

I wondered where else to look. When together
there were three of us. Martha Stewart, Joy Williams, and
myself. We didn't talk the hard times,
but we rode our bikes and called back and forth.

This hill, that deep bump, and always the clay giving over
to mud. We were pals.
We needed each other, and without a word,
We found each other.

My days were set on the challenge.
Finding Martha, Finding Joy, we three together.
We didn't talk it, we didn't cry it. we rode it out
Together in hard times.

~ Louie Galloway

PROMPT: LOOK!

Look. Listen. Taste. Smell. Touch

I don't need to Look to experience the Emerson Quartet

I don't need to Look to experience jambalaya

I don't need to Look to experience spring iris.

I don't need to Look to curl up with a friend on winter afternoons

So: life is good. Relax eyeballs. You get overworked. It's not my fault. It's this culture. Everywhere.
Here: I'll drop the lids. There... Is that better?

~ Louie Galloway

PROMPT: CELEBRATE CELIBACY

What makes sex holy? said the monk to the nun.

Don't ask me, brother. I see it coming and I run. But holy it must be or hell's overrun. The problem is it's supposed to be fun, said the nun.

Oh, said the monk, I get it now. Sex is the opposite of milking a cow. You squeeze those tits

Teats, not tits, said the nun. You monks have trouble with a nuanced tongue.

Nuanced tongue? said the monk horrified. I better be going or I'll be fried.

Good riddance, said the nun.

~ Louie Galloway

PROMPT: WHOSE GARLIC

It just sits here waiting patiently to be used.
It knows it's tough, but that just makes it tougher. "Bite me at your peril" is its mantra.
So I say, "I've been around as long as you, tough lady, and I am true to myself, none other."
Garlic replies, "I notice your hand trembles
as you pick me up. Then you reach for the blade as any aspiring chef would. I feel the pierce
in my throat, my belly. My children loosen from me, some tumbling out whole, some are only half left. You told me it would be a blessing to be of use.
So I bloomed. Now I plan to set your belly on fire."

~ Louie Galloway

PROMPT: THE LAST TIME I DANCED

The last time I danced was in Johnny's Tavern, sidling toward my partner, sexy as I am able to be these days. Letting the melodic lines lead me on. Get closer, get closer yet space to turn on a dime.

Waggling my hips (yes, I said waggling my hips)
I flash my partner a come hither look. and slightly jump to the side ... A teenage lifetime of New Orleans jazz in my imaginary ear. I could do this forever.

And my partner gives me the go ahead.
We are in great accord. And the passion of music,
and dim lights- and a bit of beer running through my body.

My partner looks at me. My partner knows where I am. After all, she's my daughter!

~ Louie Galloway

PROMPT: EARTH. AND SKY

I'm comin' home paddling lazily in water and air. It's just those eddies, those gales
those quakes that eclipse my speed

So lazily, here I cometh.

~ Louie Galloway

PROMPT: OUT OF BALANCE

When I walked out of balance, what a relief
I had been in balance for what seemed a millennium. It took
a lot out of me. But my family needed it,
the job required it, so I watched my step everyday.

Now retired, I can be true to myself, my real nature. No one
needs to know, I do get quizzical looks
at times and occasionally fall, but only on soft earth,
which receives me gently.

My vision sees beyond 3D, my nose captures new drifts,
and my ears hear the angels sing: "She is out of balance, sisters every time she takes a step.
She is creeping where the dancers make the most of any depth.
She is turning this way, that way.
And she never needs your help. Her truth is marching on.
Glory.... glory ... "

~ Louie Galloway

PROMPT: RED. DIRT. ALLEY

Red dirt alley
Clay on my shoes Earth that stays within
Clay on my
bare feet.

Where goeth thou, oh alley? To a small stream
To a faraway horizon
To the house on the corner

And who made you?
The ubiquitous buggies The clot of school children
The turn of the century mayor

Will you ever give forth a flower? Not my job, green bean.
And compromise my reputation?
Stick around, you'll see.. (stick around, get it?)

Do you know you are beautiful? I'm a classic.
Check me out in National Geographic. I do my job.

~ Louie Galloway

PROMPT: FLYING IN DREAMS
HOW TO FLY IN DREAMS
If you are relaxed,
Simply step up on the pliant air
And keep climbing
Until you can clear the tree tops
  and power lines
Then slowly pedal
  like riding a bike
Watch where you are going
Don't run into mountains
  or birds or angels.
Alternatively
Find a mob with
Flaming torches and pitchforks,
Then run.
If you are lucky
You will soon be above their reach.
Of course, if you don't
  get up some speed
they will just follow you,
poking at your heels.
I find I am most comfortable
at lower altitudes,
where I can recognize landmarks.
But on occasion
It is thrilling to soar
Straight up to the upper edge
of the atmosphere.
You gain perspective
But lose your place.

~ Katherine Greene

PROMPT: OH! THAT SWEET, SWEET ASS
Spring Fever

Longer afternoons
Giddy with sunshine and bird song
Tree pollen adding a layer of stupification
All sense of time is erased
Our bodies are uncertain of hunger
Or when to sleep
Nightfall always a surprise

~ Katherine Greene

PROMPT: I HAVE FATTENED INTO MY MOTHER'S AGE

I have fattened into my mother's age
Her bitter heart, ceaselessly hungry.
There was never enough to satisfy that piercing appetite,
Until softened by time and receding memory
She is once again secure in her mother's love
And greets me from her hospital bed
With "Happy Birthday! What kind of cake
Shall we have?"

~ Katherine Greene

PROMPT: OUT OF BALANCE

The washing machine is out of balance
Thumping as it spins
I run to sit on it
To keep it from walking
Away from the drain and plug
Across the gray slanted floor.

The washer and I
Shared the sleeping porch
Off the kitchen.
In the winter
Snow would blow through the
Lapped siding to cover my
Wool blankets with an extra layer.
It put my mother out of balance.
She grew up in cabins
And leaky old houses
And had had enough of that.
The snow never seemed to bother
The washer
And the floor was warm enough
That it melted.
I liked it.

She wanted to raise me
In a warm tight house
Not one where the book cases
Were on the north
For the extra insulation.
We moved south in the dead of winter
Into a tight brick house.
I missed the washer
And the mountains
And the snow on my blanket.

My mother was happy.
I fell out of balance.

~ Katherine Greene

PROMPT: I HELD THE CLAY
Colossus

I held the clay
With bitter hands
It softened with my tears

Crudely shaped
In awkward strands
Then curved into an ear

It's burning face
Concealed my plans
With words it could not hear.

~ Katherine Greene

PROMPT: WHISPERED INTO MY EAR
Winter Mice

The mice are writing in the ceiling again
    scratching love poems into the plaster.
The cat is an old critic
    disinclined to examine the literary attic.
The mice switch to extended sagas,
    above the desk, the kitchen, my bed.
I dream of writing scathing reviews
    and their forced relocation to a more
        temperate writers' colony.

~ Katherine Greene

PROMPT: OUR ANIMAL HAS NEVER BITTEN ANYONE BEFORE
Hospitality

Certain occupations (postman comes to mind)
And some individuals are irresistible.
It does not do
To be so toothsome
That cats and dogs
Who never bite
Want to have a taste
Of arm or leg or ankle.

When your host
Leads you into the living room
Select your seat with care.
Who knows what so-called
Innocents lurk beneath the chair
Poised to pounce
Perhaps to nip
Your gasps overspoken
By the host's
Declamation,
"Fluffy has never bitten anyone before."

Politeness dictates
That one does not bleed
On upholstery or the carpet.
But beware the eager pet
Who offers to lick the wound clean.
Safer to ask for a damp towel
And to apply direct pressure.
Be sure to excuse yourself
Before your shoes fill with blood
So as not to leave a track
As you flee.

~ Katherine Greene

PROMPT: I DREAMED YOU WERE AMONG THE DEAD

Last night I walked among the dead.
We crossed the fallow ground.
No moon lit our lively tread.
The silence was profound.

The color fled beneath our feet.
The air was cold, unmoving.
Uncertain who we were to meet,
Obscure in the proving.

We came upon the river, sere,
Carved by absent water.
Our paths diverged, it was clear
I am my mother's daughter

~ Katherine Greene

PROMPTS: SONNET, IAMBIC PENTAMETER, 14 LINES/ WHEN I SAW YOU IN THE ...

When I last saw you standing in the light
Your night gown dampened by the early dew
Your shadow dark, as day replaced the night
Our lives were so much different than we knew
Your gaze was fixed upon the distant sea
You did not turn when I called out your name
Your heart was full of hope, but not for me
Your passion deep was more than I could claim
I called again, but you did not reply
My face was hard, I could not look away
The seconds passed, I could not say goodbye.
I turned to go and hoped you'd call out "Stay"
I left you there without a single word
The silence echoes in my heart unheard.

~ Katherine Greene

PROMPTS: START OVER ON SPRING STREET / I'M WELCOME ANYTIME

Windblown seeds wide ranging
Leave without a trace

Drop, the wind receding
The cycle won't release

Sprout, then leaf, then blooming
Waiting for a breeze

Hope always surging
To an unanswered need

Random is the wind
The seed grows any place

Home is just a feeling
I see it in your face

~ Katherine Greene

PROMPT: A MOTH IN THE SALT

A mother in the salt
in the wound makes the hurt
harness memories at the table
at the table of my heart
she comes again, shaken
by her unseasonable life
which she took for herself
into her soul's cellar
in the salt, in the common sand
of the sea,
now makes me
wish for a grain of love ☺
arms reach out in a crawl
push against waves
that push back
far from shore
from even the possibility
of mother in the salt of the earth.

~ Sandy Hazlett

PROMPT: PERHAPS YOUR WOLF HAS DONE ALL SHE CAN FOR YOU & HAS MOVED ON

With my grandmother still in her belly
my wolf has moved on
the axeman gone
and left me with my hood
red mood and missing her
I set traps
springs in trees
leg hobbles
my wolf. my wolf
missing in the wood
"cunning", a word my grandmother said
for "dear" or "darling" or "quaint"
not sly like the wolf
who consumed her
but does not know
she will turn her inside out
come back to me
while the wolf has moved on
skin to sky
howling for what was left undone

~ Sandy Hazlett

PROMPT: CRACKERJACK SWEETHEART

Martin was my crackerjack sweetheart
tho his favorites were Sweet-Tarts
he had a mind quicker than carnival ducks
all lined up in a row passing at speeds
outsmarting all the shooters
Marti would let the bullets fly
crack a sugary word, give a quick hug
sending fireworks from my suddenly awakening
female lips to the top of my head
like popping corn covered in caramel ooze
and we would shmooz on the roller coaster
getting stuck on the nuts
which proved a good lesson for my future
better than I could hear from the fortune teller
dressed in spangly gauze, looking for money
but honey the future was still waiting then
and Martin, my crackerjack sweetheart,
was full of surprises.

~ Sandy Hazlett

PROMPT: IF I WERE MALE I WOULD ...

If I were mail I would send you a letter
since you put me in a box,
stamped me with your approval,
floral prints smelling of roses.

I would envelop myself
in enclosed secret space
waiting to be licked,
tongue in cheek.

The postman rings more than twice
gives me parcels and telegrams
before dogs chase him from the screen door.
You know, he told me he would take me, too.

The mail comes every day.
I wait for you, your afternoon post.
Letters, let her become
the woman she wanted to be.

Now, it is all email and text and tweet,
not as sweet as paper and pen.
On and off again, we tease with words,
call and response.

If I were male I would be you
and you would receive me in the dull day,
open me,
take up your pen.

~ Sandy Hazlett

PROMPTS: HAND ME DOWNS/ SKY AND AIR, EARTH AND WATER

Hand me down sky
blue and wanting
clear into light
present at dawn
into black night
Let me lift you up, sky

Hand me down air
in-breath peace
out-breath joy
moving, invisible
connecting all, hand to plant
Let me keep you clear, air

Hand me down earth
under foot humus soil
rich furrow of leaf and mold
keeper of bodies
bone and skin and ash
Let me be your guardian, earth

Hand me down water
cooling presence
fluid, formless
taking the shape given
the wave of sea
Let me keep you pure, water

Hand me down sky. Hand me down air and earth.
Hand me down water. Ours to keep safe, let go, hand down.

~ Sandy Hazlett

PROMPT: SCRAPS OF YOUR LIFE

The scraps of my life
frizzle in hot oil
like hush puppies
for hungry children,
anointed orts
thrown under the table,
the refuse.
I refuse to make do
but I do
as I miss the bright dinner party
through the kitchen window
and Betty sneaks hors d'oeuvres
from black, laced trays.
Alone, I watch the paper lantern lights
hanging from trees
over dancing couples
who hold each other tightly
when there is plenty of food,
the drinks keep coming,
and none of them wants for anything.

~ Sandy Hazlett

PROMPT: I LOOKED AT YOUR FACE AND SAW ...

wood for the stove,
warm promise,
pronghorn eyed,
how you run,
cougar's leap,
how you climb
roped into the neck
of the oak,
the sun circus
high falling dance
snapped up before
ground hit.
You are my net
in this aerial world,
your face maps
my celestial twin,
your embrace
an indigenous warrior.
I felt feather on fur
curtained by fire
by smoke
face to face.

~ Sandy Hazlett

PROMPT: WHAT THE MAGPIE SAW

An ornithologist said
you knew it was you
in the mirror that day.

When I looked I saw
Grandma young again
I saw yesterday's sadness
mitigated by joy waking today.

When I looked I saw
smile lines staying
at my eye corners
and furrowed brow still thinking.

But I heard
dear Mrs. Magpie
that you saw and you knew.

You saw you and knew you
which is something
I have often longed to do
to know me — not you.

To me a magpie is a magpie
and pardon me, but
any magpie will do.

Still the bird woman said
that you saw you
and knew you.

So now I think
I will try
that mirror too.

~ Joanne C. Hickey

PROMPT: WHAT SONG IS STUCK IN YOUR HEAD?
Honk for Hemp

I honked for hemp today
as instructed
by the Sunday sign-holder
who owns that corner

I honked
  not so much for hemp
  as freedom to honk
    or speak
    or dissent.

I honked
  for freedom
    to assemble
    to protest
    to care.

I honked for hemp today
  with my horn
  because I have a car with a horn
  a woman owning property
  and using her voice
    just to hear it.
And I could.

I honked for hemp today
and for upcoming elections
still hoping America
won't be bought or sold
but loved
by sign-wielding hippies
and car-owning lesbians
with voices and cars and cares.

I honked today for hemp
   and hope
   and politics
   and just to hear the sound
and see him wave.

I honked today for the USA.

~ Joanne C. Hickey

PROMPT: WRECKAGE

After the tornado
After the bulldozer
After the rebuild
Sometimes on a windy day
A little scrap of before blows by.

Or out in the garden digging
We discover forgotten objects
And the wind blows strong again.
Memory strips us bare.
The wreckage returns.

Devastation
Supposedly solved
By FEMA and good insurance
Remains long after.

Like ashes in the wind
Or weed seeds sprouting again.

~ Joanne C. Hickey

PROMPT: NOW THE EARTH WITH MANY FLOWERS PUTS ON HER SPRING EMBROIDERY - SAPPHO

Best Decorator

Mother nature is the best decorator
flinging pink whimsically
around the puff of cloud
to greet the day.

I love the celebration
in the woods following a warm rain
when tree trunks show a green side
and moss glistens moist
while fallen leaves receive
the drippings from new wet ones.

I like ripples on the pond
where the turtle dove down
Dragon flies buzzing 'round
while bullfrogs bellow
as night draws in.

I love the moonlight
filtered through winter's bare branches
as snow crunches
and simple snow whiteness resides
nestling spring wonders beneath the sheet.

I love a warm breeze
massaging my head and hair
warming every cold bone
and beckoning me to stay and play
while winter troubles fly away.

~ Joanne C. Hickey

PROMPT: SITTING IN A DARK HOUSE OF PAIN

sometimes
darkness is a welcome shroud
a graceful private deliverance
from glaring brightness
intruding uninvited
with its full spectrum
making secrets known.

sometimes
the mystery of one small flame glowing
while corners stay murky
and moonbeams matter again
brings more peace
than pain.

sometimes
feeling the depth of hurt
while it's there
and living its truth
is the only honest thing
one can choose.

sometimes
sitting silent in the dark
without pretense
but in the quiet knowing
listening to what the pain has to say
is how we finally heal.

~ Joanne C. Hickey

PROMPT: POP EXPLOSION

When the seed bangs
against the lid
shaking and jangling
letting steam escape
and fresh smell
dominate the air
my mouth waters.

When the motor whirs
and carousel creaks
until the muted
sound of popping in bag begins
then quickens and subsides.
But the timer doesn't ding
before that putrid smell
of burnt kernels mixed
with palm oil solids smoking
sets of the fire alarm
and we all leave our workstations
to assemble on the sidewalk.
I like that, too.

Or when the ticket taker
snaps up my twelve dollars
and I step through the
doors to smell movie theatre butter
and have to remind myself
it smells so much better than it is.
But I get it anyway.

Or those balls
the old ladies in our town
gave at Halloween
our town so small you could
trust homemade treats
those balls gooey
marshmallow made
dipped in butter
and wrapped in waxed paper
more interesting than delicious.
Nevertheless, a prized treat.

I do like popcorn.

~ Joanne C. Hickey

PROMPT: WRITE A SHORT POEM ABOUT A VEGETABLE OR FRUIT

Tomato
I love you
vine ripe sun
sweetened seeds
popping soft
juice dripping
stay summer
stay.

~ Joanne C. Hickey

PROMPTS: WOMEN AT THE WELL OR QUENCHING OUR THIRST/ IT WAS A HOLY MOMENT, AN UNEXPECTED MOMENT

We come
with pens and paper
quenching our thirst with words
and listening with hearts and minds
wide open.

~ Joanne C. Hickey

PROMPT: RIPE FRUIT

Bears and I
love berries
red or black or blue
in thickets
on fences
or creek banks
by the old road.

Bears and me
seek out morsels
so delightful.

I bring a bucket.
Bears don't bother.

~ Joanne C. Hickey

PROMPT: FREE WRITING IGNORING THE PROMPT
Poets

my friends gather
around the poet's campfire
to write
to sing
to laugh
to listen
Heart first and ears second.

Pens make letters
letters make words
words make lines
or sentences
until our thoughts
are reborn
from strange prompts
or dubious phrases
or last night's ecstasy
or last month's kitchen fire.

We share
with gratitude and safety
leaving judgement
in the car or on
the porch.

week by week
I float more freely
and say
Thank you.

~ Joanne C. Hickey

PROMPTS: MEN AT 50 / HER HIS PRESENCE

My mind disengages
Worn out gearshift
Pops out of first
Never made it into second.
I silently wail, I want to write –
An erudite poem, still
I would settle for
One clear crisp sentence
But my thoughts skid
Across the surface of the words
Like shiny leather shoes
Tap dancing on an icy driveway.
I brace myself against the pen
Gripping harder, bearing down I
Force each word
To writhe up out of ……….ugh…
The cramp in my foot scatters
Into a hundred tiny shards …
Use the pain! Focus., Focus!
I thrust my fingers into
That razor pile of twinges searching
For that one reflective piece.
I squint. Clarity is as elusive
as these chosen prompts.
Yet again, I am dragged
Thankfully into the vortex of
My fellow writers' energy
Swept inward, I pick up
my pen and write.

~ Nancy Hubble

PROMPTS: AS I TURNED THE CORNER, I SAW THE CAR/ PLEASE, MORE SQUEEZE/ THE LANDSCAPE OF TIME

Time is a candle,
At birth, set aflame.
Flickering shadows
Take form,
Speak their name.

Time is a landscape,
Cars turning corners
Sunrise and sunsets,
Churchyards
for mourners.

Silly!
Time doesn't exist
No tick tock or wait.
I just made up that part
When you stepped
through my gate!

~ Nancy Hubble

PROMPT: IN THE DARK

The Great and Powerful Dark
Enters without knocking
Gobbles up the colors.
Pokes out every eye.

Invites his younger brother,
The monster in the closet,
To creep around my toys
As he gives a monstrous sigh.

My house is Dark's recorder.
Every surface listens!
Folks used to joke, 'If walls had ears!'
They do! And whisper what they hear!

When Dark rolls in, the house turns on,
Inhales cold wind - breathes out dust.
My windows rattle, moan and howl.
Doors screech and growl from raspy rust

And every night the Dark will choose
Which squeals and groans he wants to play
Scratching to wake me, footsteps that shake me.
Never the voice for which I pray.

~ Nancy Hubble

BLANK PROMPT/ STANDING ABOVE THEM

Tranquil as doves,
St. Francis watches,
Standing above them.
His feeders are full.

Peaceful surround.
Chickadees calling.
Water flows freely.
Sparrows abound.

Cardinal enlightens.
His red wings flicker.
Hummingbirds' newly
Laid clutch is gone.

Still all are welcome.
Corvids will eat eggs,
Others must lay them..
Thus, life goes on.

St. Francis' blessing
Sings gracious and true.
Embrace every creature!
We all have our place here.

That rare flash of blue.
Jay Jay Jay Jay

~ Nancy Hubble

PROMPT: SNAKE/ HONEY/ THAW

Wearing steamy wet leathers,
Thaw mounts the rising sun,
Kick-starts the six legged
And cold blooded awake!
Wedge headed snakes unwind
Tongues flicker, tiger salamander growls.

Revving up the rumble roar of bees
Thaw sizzles down the creek bed
Mouth dripping honey
Challenges the four leggeds to a race
In his finest satin ribbon voice.

Riding high above the runoff,
Thaw rears up, pops a wheelie,
Howling 'Hear me , Old Coyote!'
Come out now and run!'

Skidding across the greenness,
Thaw throws sparks, begins to slide.
Laying his ride now on its side
He sets fire on the horizon's
Summer night.

~ Nancy Hubble

PROMPT: WAKING UP

Waking up
Disenchanted
Reaching out
With no hands
Growing up
In the basement
Lost the way
To make demands.

Waking up
Discontented
Acting out
With no arms
Trying to grow
Unprotected
Blind to light
And come to harm.

Sleeping here
Earth encircled
Reaching in
Through the breath
Shrinking down
Above rejected
Found my way
Accepting death

~ Nancy Hubble

PROMPTS: CORNERED EROSION/ THE DANGER OF DICTIONARIES

The danger of dictionaries
Always a burning question in our home-
How many dictionaries are enough? Or..
when does owning too many dictionaries
cause one harm?

At a yard sale, we recently bought
our third set of the Oxford English printed as
A 2 volumne set which comes in a
stand up box with its own small drawer,
the contents being a truly necessary
magnifying glass! The print is so tiny,
without the magnifier, one's squint muscles
will seize up and there will be no way to
see past your nose again, ever!
No chance one'll be able to drive a car,
which, come to think of it,
may be a blessing!

My husband, Tom, keeps a set at work,
a necessity since he's a janitor!
Our newest set and his old copy stay home.
The latter, he's had for 50+ years is retired,
only to come out on special holidays like
The Feast of the Slaughtered Innocents
Or Boxing Day, it's dry, whispery paper
thin voice singing carols and old folk songs.

The fourth family OED is our son's given
him on graduation from college by our
bookish kin, Uncle Jerry and Aunt Nan.
It lives with him, although we drop by
for a visit and tickle it a bit when
he is abroad, so it won't be lonely.

Then there is the Behemoth Dictionary,
A Giant Roamer which
repeatedly appears to be canoodling
with the phone book pile. Since it weighs
about as much as a small sow or a mastiff,
we must be careful when pushing in a chair
that the Roamer might currently reside on as
a sprained back or hamstring is the
most likely outcome. Our kitchen chairs
were once sturdy oak school desks, now with desk
sawn off at the seat. They were acquired after
husband and son regularly destroyed all
our old kitchen chairs
(They are a pair of long legged leaners –both!).
The desk chair also comes with a handy
book shelf underneath ....
where the Roamer often lurks.
In deference to its size, I have made several
attempts to give it a single 'nest' on a table all
its own to no avail. Move furniture at your
peril in the Kellogg-Hubble household.

One of the small bevy of 'even older' dictionaries,
a 1930s Webster and two very old Collegiates
manage to crawl out onto the floor on
occasion and have been known to trip an
unsuspecting late night sleepwalker in the dark.
And though I have not been able to find many
'Modern' words in our bevy of books, we are loth
to retire them to the Salavation Army, fearful
their age will mean consignment to the dust bin
rather than a respectful place in a new home!

When I was very small, age three,
a traveling dictionary salesman
came to our farmhouse door, sold my mother
a set of enormous book covers for an
unabridged Webster's and the complete set of As.
Every month thereafter, we received
The Letter of the Month for $1.44.
Once a day, we read a page together.
Mother would read the word, I'd
Repeat it and the definition too and
As the dictionary grew in size, I learned
The mysteries of 'abaci', the rhythmic
Beauty of 'nevertheless.'
The danger came when I first started school.
In kindergarten, I was a little freak.
Later too, I found - to play with words
Was better than eating cake though others
Thought I must be daft - make no mistake
I wouldn't change my life for any other.
Dictionaries always have a home,
Thanks be to mother,
With me and my beloved word-smith mate.

~ Nancy Hubble

PROMPTS: SALT & PEPPER/ GENIUS IS 99% PERSPIRATION / TEAKETTLE

Genius is 99% perspiration and 1% Viscera

The checkerboard is set up with vodka shots
So put the teakettle on, honey
Cause I just love to hear that kettle scream,
While we blow away our troubles
In vodka jumps and king-me bubbles.

My, my that was a wild game.
Let's trade the teakettle for Little Richard.
I'll put the record on- just got a new needle.
Sharp!

Sit yourself down- right over here by me.
Ohhwee, I LOVE your buttocks.
Because they are sooo firm,
I'm going to name one 'teen'
and the other will be 'ager '
In deference to our longevity
And how you make me feel!

Now it may be gutsy
but what do you say we work up a sweat?
Rubbing our salt and peppers together!
Genius, eh?

~ Nancy Hubble

PROMPTS: THE ONE THAT GOT AWAY/ TABS/ GLUED TOGETHER

Monster me
Out of parts
The Secret Garden,
Jayne Eyre and
The dictionary

Whenever, she,
Poked out her head,
In a roiling storm
lightning strikes,
So I made a fakir
my golem self.
simulacrum as
ever a slave

Then along came
Who renovated
Brave Voices
The 'who' I am
Embraced! What
Me that can be
and no longer
for I am taking
to grow, to write,

Glued together
I found in books.
Funny papers,
Reader's Digest
Unabridged.

The real me
Color me dead
of thunder and
switches and belts
who didn't feel
A non-sassy
Well behaved
Should need to be!

a reclamation crew.
folks like me!
calling, 'All for one!'
was built anew -
pieces of the infant
found are nurtured
can I be a monster me
my own space
to love to be!

~ Nancy Hubble

PROMPT: TERMINAL NOSTALGIA

Is this the nostalgia that you feel
As you enter the terminal one last time,
With your hopeful two-way ticket
Straight to death?
This would be nostalgia
Greater than any other
Remembering even insignificant days,
Difficult nights. The wins and losses
(With loss winning) Would be pleasure
Laced with pain. You want the natural world!
You want the body! What you already know,
However flawed and sticky.
You will remember the bird-song Dawns
Of kindergarten.
Snakes swimming in streams
Moonlit kisses, primal embraces, howling.
You will think of Music, places, people
People who still love you.
(How can they do without you?)
Ready or not, here comes the train!

~ Dixie Lubin

PROMPT: YOU DO NOT HAVE TO BE WHAT YOU ARE NOT

You do not have to be what you are not.
What you are is more than sufficient.
It is a whole truth, individual
As a pebble or shell. Chips and cracks
The odd and awkward growth – those
Discolorations
Only add to your value.

You don't have to be what you are not
You come from Divine Mystery
With your own destiny, your own
Gifts, ready to hum to those around you,
Fully ready to love – in that particular
Body /soul you were given.

You do not have to be what you are not.
Lay down the burden of opinion and expectation.
Wrap your arms around you, feel blood
Surging in your veins, sing
Your own song. Listen. Give thanks.
Walk into the future with your arms
Wide open, with your mind wide open

~ Dixie Lubin

PROMPTS: MY CHOSEN LANDSCAPE / BETWEEN SEASONS

If only I could choose
A time, a place, a season
Beyond reason – a magic land
In which to stand.
It could be here and now
Or maybe here and then.
Imagine eastern Kansas one hundred years
Ago, or in some vastly unknown future.
I know there would be more birds,
More trees, less words.
I see the Flint Hills
Vast sea of green
Bison herds and small holdings
Villages with sun power, wind power.
Empowered people
Powerful children
Playing music, working
Under a clear, endless sky.

~ Dixie Lubin

PROMPT: LANDSCAPE OF MY HEART
Flint Hills

I aspired to Himalayas
But was gifted with flint hills,
Gently rolling, rough edges
Blurred by time and the earth's turning.
Underneath, bedrock breaks down
Nourishing crop after crop
Of brilliant green grass, insects, animals.
Given rain, the feral poetry of flowers.

The humans fence and parcel me out
But I tell you, the land is one.
Long, flowing presence
That knows nothing of time.
Always I am dancing the ancient cycles.
Again I die, again I am reborn.
I live to greet the sun, bask
In moonlight's blessings.
Elemental, my soul, water and my spirit, air,
I myself the ground of being
Full of primal wonder and sorrow.
Fires transform me in their season
Clearing underbrush of chatter and confusion.
Then once again, I fully awaken
To the love of nature, to the nature of love.

~ Dixie Lubin

PROMPT: YOU CAN'T GO BACK

You can't go back, the past is gone
The future a shaky branch eager to leaf out
Or possibly break—all you have
Is the now of now ... tenuous, alive, breathing.
You can't go back to where you were
That person is gone, a memory.
The question is always who are you
Right now? Does light shine through you?
Is your consciousness contained in your brain?
Is it also in that lizard, that sky, the leaf mold underfoot?

Are you pierced through in this holy moment?
Once again, you have the choice
To be more or less than you were,
The choice to embrace your divinity
So that time passing is just one dimension
In the infinite sea of possibility.
You can't go back, a blessing, really:
You are free now and you can go.

~ Dixie Lubin

PROMPT: THE YOUNG

Poignant in their awkward beauty
So ignorant they are followed by angels
Thinking they know the score…
How to be hot, and cool, and bored
How to go to the head of the class
"Are they looking at my ass?"
hearts shattering easily
like broken mirror glass
then picking up the pieces
bouncing back again.
So very interested in the forbidden
But catch them in the act, they'll say
They were only kidding.
Living on their machines
Lost in the culture's crazy dreams
Innocent at heart, so eager
To start, to really start.

~ Dixie Lubin

PROMPT: VISION

This woman's big – she dances
With confidence and joy, she's not
Young; her neck says she's bent before
And not just once. You wouldn't
Call her pretty, she is beautiful as a holy person.
Her head expanding into light
Big hands gesturing and freeing
She is singing the mantra
She is dancing the mantra
She is chanting in the green light
The mantra of "I am."

Sister, you are grey, yet
Too radiant to be a ghost
You are made of blue clay and starlight
Which life do you speak from?
My own beautiful sister is long dead
In life she loved, she wrote,
She danced as you do
She sang the mantra 'I am'.

~ Dixie Lubin

PROMPT: BESIDE THE RIVER OF THE DANCE, THE TREES SEEK

The dance, flowing like a river
On the stage of space and time
The dancer, incandescent, a small
Bright flame burning up invisible
Barriers to beauty –
As she moves, flickers, shifts
Through levels of consciousness
Evocative, provocative, eternal
As earth moving in space

She is merciful, reaches inside us
Releasing the wetlands of our thirsty souls
Around us, birds fly up by hundreds
Scribing calligraphic messages into the sky
On the banks of the Kaw, trees drink
Earth wisdom, roots soaking up nourishment,
Questioning nothing, while the dancer
Straddles dimensions, allows us,
For a moment, to exist without thought.

~ Dixie Lubin

PROMPTS: WORD SALAD / CONFESSION

I confess, oh confusion, I have done it.
I have oranges and pickles, not twice
Or one hundred, but beautifully
Every shameful day! Not the airplane,
Not the girl's mooning glance, her
Nipples and grandpa, shooting cow milk
In my mouth, into me, mi, me little,
Straight from the teat, that tittle-tattle…
Don't tell! Don't tell! I confess, sister,
Father/mother superior, I do it all
The time (not sorry, not worried yet,
Just feels so good) my salad waiting,
Words to eat, and never the people –
The people were eaten by someone,
Someone else! I, snot-nosed
Butterfingers, but cannibal – I
Don't think so, what do I do, what
Don't I do – no matter! You there,
In your underwear, what about
Your thin sins? I don't believe your
God. Your sin, my shin, just shut up!
My world has red sun, blue son. When
Both are up, all acts of love and pleasure
Are purple, just like cabbage. You think
You're so smart, my heart is a fist
Size bruise and I can't dance any more.
I used to cut the rug with scissors,
Mama hit me for that.

~ Dixie Lubin

PROMPT: WRITE A POEM ABOUT A SPECIFIC TREE

Cottonwood Sonata

Cottonwood likes to stand by the river
Sinking root toes into running water
Grows fast, tall and sturdy, leaves all aquiver
Holds up her branches, the sun's fine daughter.

Cottonwood makes sticky buds in the spring
Magical buds for making a potion
Carries them high so you can't reach a thing
Plays with the wind, and murmurs in motion.

Cottonwood dreams by the stream in the heat
Seeds floating in air, small gossamer stars
Her leaves, great green heart, their rustling so sweet
You start to dream too, of a life with no wars.

To love cottonwood, go lie on the shore
South wind will whisper – be still to know more.

~ Dixie Lubin

PROMPT: ELIMINATE

Use it to describe refined sugar, coffee,
or animal protein I removed from my diet.
It works for exercise, although I didn't
have it to eliminate anyway.
Use it to discuss a policy that won't work,
a police suspect who's been ruled out,
or a boyfriend you no longer wish to date.

It works for the red dress left
at the store because it doesn't fit right.
But let's not use it to describe
the person dying in the street,
the one a government or police
state threw a weapon in front
of as an excuse to watch them bleed out.

People aren't eliminated,
human life is too precious
to equate it to taking out the trash.

~ Ronda Miller

PROMPT: DAD

Sometimes you skip over
the things in therapy that
are the reason you are in therapy,
but the man standing silently
invisible by the door,
holding his head in his hands,
is my Dad and he can't speak
so I can't speak, so I sit
through that session and the next
and the next mute and muted.

I dream of my decapitated dad,
who is the dad of my childhood
reality, even before he died.
His was the face cut from the boxes
of photographs of my mom,
siblings and me.

The headless fatherly man
was the man who kidnapped me and moved
every month to keep from getting caught.
We were hungry and scared and freezing
and I got tired of hearing the beatings
of children and women through paper thin walls,
never knowing, not knowing,
did they hear mine too?

But I know he had a head,
he laid it in my lap one time
when I was five and I touched
his beautiful auburn hair,
smoothed it away from his face.

I saw it again at 19
when I tracked him down.
This was years after Kansas
decided Colorado wasn't
the place I should live and
my father should live
in prison for a time.

The last time I saw his head
it was in a coffin,
after his murder,
but I think it was connected
to his body.
I didn't check.
I can't be certain.

In my dreams,
waking and sleeping,
it is the headless dad I see.
He stabs my grandfather
to death for molesting me.
He looks over my shoulder
as I brush my teeth,
he appears in closets and
the dark shadowy bottom
of swimming pools.

He is always watching,
looking out for me,
just as I am always looking,
watching,
waiting for him
to give me permission
to speak.

~ Ronda Miller

PROMPT: HOSPICE

we refused them
the last few drops
of water knowing
it was all that was
keeping them alive.

how much longer
it would have added
to their hearts' beating
we had no way of knowing.

it was the knowledge
that it added time + agony
to our own days and nights,
not theirs, that we feared.

one asked for milk,
how he longed
for the sweetness
of the taste.

the connection
of being joined
to his mother
didn't cross our minds
until he was gone.

It was then
we realized
it wouldn't have
made a difference
in his pneumonia;
in anything except
a small pleasure
we had no right to deny.

~ Ronda Miller

PROMPT: SHE SAYS

She doesn't dream.
Each afternoon I ask, hopeful,
she as despondent as I by her response.
"Not of ponies, a unicorn, white kittens?" I ply.
She shakes her head side to side.
Full lips whisper, "No," so quietly that I'm lip reading.

During the day, she shares her tears,
tells me how badly she misses her mom
who lives behind bars.
Her older brother, who has
somehow transformed into her
baby brother, she cries for him too.
They have different fathers.
His came for him, hers has not.

Today I decide to change things.
I don't ask her if she had a dream, I know she did.
I know she does every afternoon and night.
They are nightmares, filled with a loss so dark
they can't be shared in light of day,
can't be spoken, can not be remembered.
They are felt so far inside there are no words to share.

I sit beside her, rub her back.
her dark eyes open, flutter shut, reopen.
"Let me tell you about your dream," I say.
"You were riding a rainbow unicorn
with a fuzzy, white kitten in your pocket.
She kept peeking her big bright blue eyes
out to tell you where to go.
You went all the way to the moon and back.
I saw you there myself."
Her face relaxes, and she smiles.

~ Ronda Miller

PROMPT: GEESE

circle around,
fly backwards,
fail to synchronize,
flail and squawk,
eventually fall
away into space,
their instincts
as confused as my own.

This year an antichrist
strides, legs long enough
to reach Kansas from D.C.,
or is that New York?

Native Americans fight
for clean water rights
the world over, stand
their ground as others
around me shrink and smirk,
shirk family duties.

How do we triage
those we love?
Why can't we inconvenience
ourselves, downsize our homes,
or simply ask that aged
parent for a loan,
live together as one?

I keep faith/presence
with like minded people,
promise myself
to continue the fight,
search the sky for geese,
who by instinct,
know where they're going,
take flight,
and so do I.

~ Ronda Miller

PROMPT: I STAND

I turn on the water faucet.
Not a day goes by that I don't
think about how blessed
I am to have running water,
clean water, water to drink,
to cook with, to wash myself
and my clothing, to flush
what my body can't use away.

I think about how much water
it takes to fill your body and mine,
and how it flows through us without
our thinking about it.

My dreams are about water,
drowning in it, close to boats
that float just out of reach.

I dream of Water Protectors,
think how sacred they
are to our way of life,
to staying alive.
I'm a water sign. I've always
felt the burden, the duty,
the heaviness of carrying water
to crops, to livestock,
to the garden patch.

Sometimes the weight
of my own water
is too heavy to carry alone.

I've felt the joy of water,

the cooling of a fevered brow,
walking through it, submerging
myself within, watching it as rainbow
lift against autumn sky.

Emotions flow through us,
fill our vessels, escape
our eyes as water droplets.

I remember the joy of carrying
my children, filled with their own water,
inside of me. Then my water
broke and they carried their own
water forward and away from me.
They were able to live because
of breast milk I made from my water.

I watch in silence as the Water Protectors
are hurt by their water, our water,
a weapon again them.

~ Ronda Miller

PROMPT: SEVEN OF PENTACLES

She stands by the closet
Looking at racks of business wear,
Piles of yoga pants with
Pills and tiny holes,
Her ex-husband's ex-T-shirts,
Vacuum cleaner parts,
A basket of cat toys.
She shuts the door.
The mirror with the HRC sticker
In the bottom right corner hands an
Image back to her,
Pre-pregnancies, pre-desk jobs, pre-
Stauffers family-sized lasagnas.
The girl in the mirror leans
Sideways, arms overhead.
She wears a hand-me-down
Leotard that her
Mother doesn't approve of and the
Record player needle skips.
She deepens her stretch with
Fluid arms reaching out like
Tree limbs. Birds perch
On her fingers and dandelions
Sprout up at her feet.
The mirror is a fast-running creek.
She sways in sunlight streaming
From an empty ceiling fan socket.
She blazes as she spins and swings
and grows and grows and
Grows, taller than her
House by the railroad tracks,
Taller than the steeple at
Freewill Baptist, taller

Than the new Holiday Inn Express.
Nothing can touch her.
She grabs fistfuls of painted
Sky, blue running
Down her hair, her
Long meadowed legs.
She swallows a star, crunches
Venus between her teeth.
What woman doesn't have a universe
For a belly? Who isn't
Born a girl wary of roots,
Firm-footed on a precipice?
Contrary.
Just waiting for the right time
To jump. What woman,
If she opens her eyes,
Can't catch her precious self?

~ Amy Nixon

PROMPT: I MADE A DECISION

I made a decision
Not to feel everything.
I've felt everything for so long
Watched too many faces,
Read too many lips.
No words spoken,
Too many heard.

~ Gail Curtis Sloan

PROMPT: I LIE SLEEPLESS

I lie sleepless, think of the eagles soaring
On winter afternoons above the Kaw.
How do they know when it's time,
That their mate will return?

A congress of moon-lit seagulls shares this inland lake with me tonight.
They know the answer, fly a thousand miles to slake their needs on salt-marsh deltas.
But I know them, they keep their counsel, they will not tell.

~ Gail Curtis Sloan

PROMPT: IMMORTALITY

Maybe this isn't the prompt we heed?
Ignore its first two letters, tear away the "t"
And morality, the word de jour, appears
With sickeningly precise regularity.
Seasoned with ignorance, tainted by fear
It curdles sermons and issues edicts.
Blaspheming all loving Gods
Bludgeoning all who disagree.

~ Gail Curtis Sloan

PROMPT: CHILDREN GROW UP, LEAVE

Children grow up – leave
Who knew my heart
Would refuse to down-size?

~ Gail Curtis Sloan

WRITING WITHOUT USING THE PROMPT

Sailing home
The shortest route
Is seldom the quickest.
Storms blow from nowhere
Reefs hide below the shimmer.
We find ourselves alone
Together.

~ Gail Curtis Sloan

PROMPTS: IT'S SIMPLE/
IT'S ALWAYS SOMEONE ELSE UNTIL IT'S NOT

Simple isn't always easy
For someone else.
"Just eat less", "Try harder"
"Always drive defensively"
"Don't think about it" - "It will get better"
"They'll grow up and make you proud."
Comes the day when you are the someone else
Then simple is impossible.

~ Gail Curtis Sloan

PROMPTS: WHAT I HEAR IN SILENCE / LET US HAVE A MOMENT OF SILENCE

Feel the breeze
Miles away from cars
Miles away from people
Wait, listen, for the moment.

Sounds of water.
Sounds of birds,
Insects,
Trees.
Sounds of airplanes
Wait.

Silence never comes.
The moment a delusion
The sounds of the earth
Abound.

~ Libeth Tempero

PROMPTS: WAITING FOR A CHANGE / CHANGE WILL COME

Waiting for a change
Knowing it will come
No matter what is done
Even if I run.

Waiting for a change
And missing what it is
Thinking I'm the same
Gravity always wins

Waiting for a change
Life is all brand new
They all would tell me when
But did not say what's true.

Waiting for a change
Freedom in the form
The person newly born
Unto the final grave.

~ Libeth Tempero

PROMPT: WHEN DRAGONS FLY

Unfettered
When dragons fly
Over the mossy pond
When the days are soft
The evenings warm

When the night is full
Of starry light
The fireflies
Echo their delight

When fairies dance
Beneath the moon
Look for me
By the ancient ruin

I'll be dancing
To songs, unsung
To harps, unstrung
To bells, unrung

~ Libeth Tempero

We would love to hear from you!
Please contact the poets at:
ANAMCARA PRESS LLC
P.O. Box 442072, Lawrence, KS 66044
https://anamcara-press.com

CONTRIBUTORS:

Deborah Altus
Deborah has lived, loved and played in Lawrence for the past 36 years where she likes to run with the Mad Dogs and hang out with her Kawsmology study group. She's also a professor at Washburn University.

Micki Carroll
Micki Carroll has taught and written about conflict, diversity, and community for over 20 years. Carroll published her father's WWII photographs & detailed his POW experiences in her 2016 book, *A Wyoming Cowboy in Hitler's Germany*. Carroll has also authored several children's books including, *The Tree Who Walked Through Time*, *The Boy Whose Branches Reached the Stars*, and *Spiders Dance*. She blogs at: https://maureencarroll.com/.

Iris Craver
Iris Craver enjoys leading creative writing groups in the community, at the library, local treatment centers, the county jail and through the Parks and Recreation department. She is a nationally certified poetry therapist. Iris is Professor Emeritus at Washburn University. She has recently published a book titled *Write to the Source ~ A Journaling Guide for Recovery* which is available through the Raven bookstore, the Washburn University bookstore, and Amazon.

Kimberli Eddins
Kimberli Eddins currently resides in Tucson, AZ loving the warmth and bright sun. She works as an Early Childhood teacher. Loves making art, writing poetry with friends, reading, and taking walks in the desert as well as watching movies and thrift store shopping.

Louie Galloway
Louie Galloway grew up in rural Louisiana and New Orleans. She received her doctorate from Boston University and taught at Massachusetts College of Art, where she is professor emerita. She now lives in Lawrence, KS where she walks on the levee of the Kansas River. She is grateful for her family, her many friends in many places, the women's movement, and her mother.

Katherine Greene
Katherine Greene is a retired law librarian living in North Lawrence with her husband Dan Bentley and several cats in the middle of a beautiful garden. She began writing poetry decades ago. Second Sunday Goes Fourth gives her the space and time to practice her love of poetry and word play.

Sandy Hazlett

Sandy Hazlett's poems have been published in *Coal City Review, I-70 Review, Quattrocento*, and in *365 Days, A Poetry Anthology*. Poems from her chapbook, *The Prom Dress Room* were featured in *Coal City Review 36:2015*. The *Prom Dress Room* was published by Anamcara Press in 2015 as a fundraiser for The Social Service League of Lawrence, Kansas. Sandy lives and works on her farm in rural Lawrence, Kansas.

Joanne C. Hickey

Joanne Hickey loves hearing, writing, reciting and reading poetry, especially writing poetry in the company of friends. She inherited the love of poetry from her mom and grandpa.

Nancy Hubble

Calling Lawrence home for the last 50 years, Nancy luckily stumbled into an enclave of poets, artists and writers who have encouraged her to do likewise and, finding herself in good company, she has. She has taught a variety of subjects in three alternative school settings and writing in ESL at KU. Her publications include art, poetry and prose in *Wakarusa Wetlands, Begin Again, To the Stars Through Difficulty, Tallgrass Voices, Hot Summer Nights*, various Guidry & Lubin Zines, *I 3 Dead Birds*, and *Kansas Curiosities 2*. Nancy has one chapbook with CD, *Dharma Dog*.

Dixie Lubin

Dixie Lubin is a longtime Lawrence resident who has been writing and reading poetry since childhood. She facilitates writing and creativity groups. Her poems are in several publications: *The Carbon Chronicles-Harvest of Arts poets 1992-1996, Kaw, Kaw, Kaw, as the Poets Fly from Lawrence, Kansas,* (a CD), and two books edited by Caryn Miriam Goldberg, *Begin Again—150 Kansas Poems,* and *To the Stars Through Difficulty—A Kansas Renga.* Dixie and Fred Lubin also published a chapbook, *Slightly Tilting Toward the Void/Rabid Doggerel.* Dixie is also an outsider artist.

Gail Curtis Sloan

Gail Curtis Sloan lives in Lawrence, KS. She is a sailor, shepherd, professor and feminist who considers journaling an indispensable survival skill. She and her husband Tom share a passion for family, farming, and moderate Kansas politics.

Ronda Miller

Ronda Miller is a Life Coach who works with clients who have lost someone to homicide. She is a Fellow of The Citizen Journalism Academy, World Company, and she created poetic forms loku and ukol. She was the co-chair, along with Caryn Mirriam-Goldberg, for the Transformative Language Arts Conference at Unity Village September, 2015. Miller is State President of The Kansas Authors Club (2018-2019). Her three books of published poetry include: *Going Home: Poems from My Life, MoonStain, and WaterSigns.*

Amy Nixon
Amy Nixon is a writer, artist, and animal lover.

Libeth Tempero
Libeth Tempero is coalescing a very scattered life into one of being a writer. By education she is a sociologist, mechanical engineer, and nearly a biochemist. By interests she has made art in stained glass, water color, and acrylic. Her interest in history or more exactly her story has been augmented by learning to make bobbin lace, knit, and sew as well as gardening. Currently she is nearing the end of editing her novella set in Ireland complete with fairies and religion. It is about a girl orphaned by the potato famine. Libeth hopes to self-publish after having been told that historical fiction does not have fairies. She manages to stay just outside whatever box presents itself.

Tim Passmore
Originally from Belleville, Kansas, Tim is a photographer and humorist. He studied at Kansas State University and Cloud County Community College. A former educator and Peace Corps volunteer, he is now retired from Pawnee Mental Health Services. He presently lives in Talmo, Kansas.

www.ingramcontent.com/pod-product-compliance
Lightning Source LLC
Chambersburg PA
CBHW021154080526
44588CB00008B/336